Track& Field

LeRoy T. Walker

12/15/89
Best Wishes
L.T. Walker

A GUIDE FOR THE SERIOUS COACH AND ATHLETE

A Sports Publication By

The Athletic Institute
200 Castlewood Street
North Palm Beach, FL. 33408

Library of Congress Catalog Card Number 82-74328
ISBN 0-87670-070-9

A WORD FROM THE PUBLISHER

THIS SPORTS PUBLICATION, is but one item in a comprehensive list of sports instructional aids, such as video cassettes, 16mm films, 8mm silent loops and filmstrips which are made available by The Athletic Institute. This book is part of a master plan which seeks to make the benefits of athletics, physical education and recreation available to everyone.

The Athletic Institute is a not-for-profit organization devoted to the advancement of athletics, physical education and recreation. The Institute believes that participation in athletics and recreation has benefits of inestimable value to the individual and to the community.

The nature and scope of the many Institute programs are determined by a Professional Advisory Committee, whose members are noted for their outstanding knowledge, experience and ability in the fields of athletics, physical education and recreation.

The Institute believes that through this book the reader will become a better performer, skilled in the fundamentals of this fine event. Knowledge and the practice necessary to mold knowledge into playing ability are the keys to real enjoyment in playing any game or sport.

Howard J. Bruns
President and Chief Executive Officer
The Athletic Institute

Dustin A. Cole
Executive Director
The Athletic Institute

CONTENTS

SECTION I:

The Sprints

SECTION II:

Relay Racing

SECTION III:

The Hurdles

SECTION IV:
Distance Running

SECTION V:
The Horizontal Jump

SECTION VI:
The Vertical Jumps

SECTION VII:
The Throws

SHOT PUT

DISCUS

SECTION VIII:
Building a Training Program

SECTION I

The Sprints

THE SPRINTS

The sprints include those races in which the competitor runs distances up to 400 meters. Indoor competition includes races as short as 45 meters. When Lee Evans set the World's Record in the 400 meters in the Olympic Games in Mexico in 1968 in the time of 43.8, this was indeed a sprint effort. Some writers contend that man can maintain full speed for only 15 seconds, after which he begins to slow down. In the 100- to 400-meter dashes there is obviously some deceleration. Dr. Arthur Steinhous, a noted physiologist, once stated that "the competitor was capable of running a 100-yard dash in one breath." He further stated that 200 meters was the maximum distance that man could run at full speed. This statement is probably true in terms of one's definition of full speed.

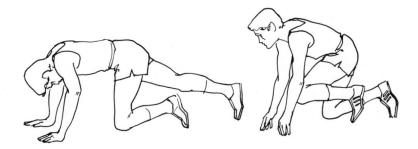

Sprinting Basics

Sprinters come in all shapes and sizes. Some are tall, others are short, some are strong and powerful, others are lean. Sprinters possess some combination of the characteristics of an explosive start, great acceleration, pickup, or tremendous lift at the finish. However, there is no exact mold of a sprinter. Howard Drew, Ira Murchison, Ed Roberts are examples of small men who performed outstandingly in the sprints. Mel Patton, Tommy Smith, Larry Black, Valerie Borzov, Bob Hayes, are examples of tall, powerful, long-striding sprinters. All of the above sprinters did not demonstrate equal ability in the start, acceleration, the pickup, or the lift. Each, however, possessed some combination of the characteristics which resulted in a great sprint effort.

There are some basics which describe a sprint effort:

1. Regardless of the type of starting position used, sprinters usually attain highly similar horizontal velocities over the first five or six strides.

2. It is generally agreed that in the 100-meter sprint maximum velocity is reached somewhere between 40 and 60 meters from the start and that very few sprinters can maintain this maximum velocity all the way to the finish line.

3. A track position very close to the vertical is associated with the high-velocity sprint.

4. It is clear that during the first few strides from the starting line more time is spent in the support phase to prepare the body than is spent in the flight phase.

5. At 50 meters, the support time for the sprinter is less than 50% of total stride time. This is a reason for the demand of excellent drive against the surface of the track.

6. Stride time changes very little as the sprinter increases horizontal velocity. It is obvious, therefore, that stride length has to increase.

7. Changes in stride length appear to be minimal after a velocity of approximately 7 meters per second. It is generally agreed that at the high velocities of running stride rate changes more than does stride length.

8. It is important to control stride length because longer strides take more time than shorter strides, mainly due to an increase in flight time.

9. A considerable variation in sprint pattern and techniques can be seen in top sprinters. Therefore, there cannot be one single model of stride perfection that is suited to all sprinters. Not even all sprinters on the same team can be forced into the same mold.

Training Format for the Complete Sprinter

It is essential to develop an efficient, comfortable running style. Three points are important.

1. Utilize minimum body lean — only enough forward lean to assure proper track surface reaction.
2. Develop maximum control stride lengths.
3. Develop highest possible stride frequency.

In order to achieve the correct and most efficient running style, the question naturally arises: are sprinters born? Some experts contend that sprinters may be born because there is strong evidence to support the position that stride frequency is inborn. However, there is evidence which suggests that proper training can improve stride frequency without sacrificing stride length. This position is advanced by coaches who use downhill run to increase leg reflex and towing of athletes in an attempt to increase stride frequency.

It is probably of even greater significance to develop confidence in the ability to sustain and to repeat short and long sprints with minimum deceleration. A training format which is based upon repeat efforts at control speeds is the key to developing the complete sprinter.

The cycle and reacceleration concept of training consists of two basic factors in developing the complete sprinter. The material below illustrates what is required as a means of projecting the cycle and reacceleration program. The first procedure involves dividing the track or a running area into four equal 100-meter segments.

Pole Progression and Regressions

Beginning each 100 meters represents one pole. In this format the sprinter will run from one to five poles, skipping the four pole segment. Run one pole, jog one pole. Run two poles, jog two poles, etc. . . . The pole progression and regressions are completed in cycles.

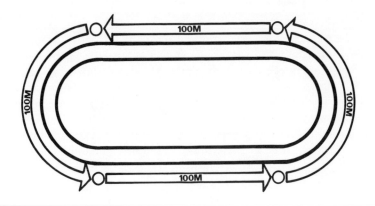

One cycle may constitute a series of pole sprints from one through five, or the cycle may include the progressions of one through five and the regressions of five back to one. The time segment is determined as follows and is based on an increased percent of time being allowed for each pole above the individual's normal time to run 100 meters, 200 meters or 400 meters.

Each sprinter's time for the various segments is determined by adding time to his/her previous best time recorded. If there is no record, estimate a time. The following illustrates the principles.

1 pole (100 meters) = best 100m time + 30-35% of time added.
2 poles (200 meters) = best 200m time + 34-45% of time added.
3 poles (300 meters) = best 400m time — 10%.
5 poles (500 meters) = best 400m time + 50% of time added.

In the 1 and 2 pole sprints, allow the higher percent and reduce the percent as the condition of the athlete improves.

Best Time

Male	100m 10.0 ± 35% (3.5s) 1 pole 13.5	
Female	100m 12.0 ± 35% (4.2) 1 pole 16.2	
Male	200m 22.0 ± 45% (9.9) 2 poles 31.9	
Female	200m 25.0 ± 45% (11.3) 2 poles 36.3	
Male	400m 50.0 ± 10% (5.0) 3 poles 45.0	
Female	400m 55.0 - 10% (5.5) 3 poles 49.5	
Male	400m 50.0 ± 50% (25.0) 5 poles 1:15	
Female	400m 55.0 ± 50% (27.5) 5 poles 1:22.5	

There are two additional exercises in the sprint format. One is to split the three poles into a one- and two-pole sprint, split the five pole into a two- and three-pole split in order to permit a slightly faster pace. For example, the three-pole split for the times indicated above would mean the one pole would be run in 13.5 with a jog and the 2 pole would be run in 31.9. These times could be rounded off to fourteen seconds and thirty-two seconds. However, in the split pole drill one could reduce the time by five-tenths of a second in order to demand a reacceleration by the sprinter which is a very essential drill to produce top quality sprinting. In splitting the five pole according to the times indicated above, the sprinter would run two poles in 31.9, jog two poles then run three poles in 45 seconds. Again, in this drill the times could be reduced by five-tenths of a second because of the fact that the pole cycle is not being run.

The purpose of the cycle format is to permit the sprinter to develop a dual system both aerobic and anaerobic. As indicated by Steinhous, if an individual can sprint full effort only fifteen seconds which will completely use all the phosphagen available — "the quick energy phase" — there must be developed a second system to carry a sprint action beyond seventy-five or eighty meters.

The Start

In the short sprint race, the winner is often determined in the first five to twenty meters. Among the several prerequisites for an effective start is the characteristic of "mental toughness" in approaching the starting line. Mental toughness is not suddenly generated as a sprinter waits for the starter's command. The sprinter must cultivate it through hours of practice. It comes as a sprinter develops a belief in his/her ability, gains confidence in the integrity of starters, and develops the power to concentrate.

Mental Toughness in the Starting

The sprinter's belief in his/her ability to start with the very best comes with the mastery of starting technique. It is very helpful to begin with the take-your-mark command when all in the immediate environment is quiet. Good sprinting involves preparation before the initial phase of the start.

The sprinter should be made aware of improvements as practice takes place so that he or she will begin to be "mentally tough" as the starting line is approached. He must be constantly aware of improvement and reaction time and an explosiveness from the blocks. The sprinter should understand that it is not the starter's responsibility to see that all runners start together. The starter's only obligation is to see that all runners are motionless before the gun sounds. Whether or not all runners start together is the responsibility of each sprinter on the line.

It is important for the sprinter to develop confidence in the starter and in his/her own ability. Mental toughness is lost whenever the sprinter begins to wonder if the starter will permit a roll, or in some way give an opponent an advantage. This confidence is developed at starting practice sessions. There must not be any forward motion before or even at the sound of the gun. The athlete should strive to avoid a sloppy start at any time during practice.

7

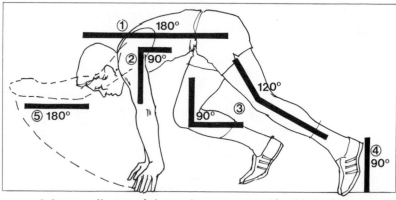

It is generally agreed that sprinters vary considerably in their starting techniques. It is also generally agreed that the leg length and other factors will determine foot spacing. There are five basic body angles as the sprinter is on the mark, takes the position and leaves the starting blocks. These five angles of accommodation are: (1) head, shoulder, hip alignment — 180 degrees, (2) the arms, shoulder, angle with the track surface — 90 degrees, (3) the lower leg and thigh position against the two pedals of the starting block — 90 degrees for the front, 120 degrees for the rear leg, (4) placement of the foot as it leaves the rear pedal in relationship to the finish line — 90 degrees, (5) the lead arm as it drives through in a relationship with the track surface — 180 degrees.

Obviously these angles may never be fully achieved but the most efficient start is measured in terms of near approximation to the desired angles. Furthermore, it should be noted that sprinters may present different angles of accommodation because of body alignment and size and still all may be very effective. The sprinter should let the stop watch determine the effectiveness of the angles and the quality of the start. There is no longer a standard of inches which can be used to describe proper foot spacing according to height and size. Foot spacing in the blocks is influenced by the mechanics of the start and the results expected. The taller the runner the farther from the starting line should be the front foot. The distance chosen will influence the comfort of the runner and the appropriate angles made by the thigh and lower leg as described above. The block spacing between the feet would influence the angle of the rear leg and the tension and the power point.

Two frequently made errors should be avoided. One is the error of crowding the starting line; this leaves the front leg in a position which dictates an upward thrust at the gun. The second error is the block spacing which encourages a high hip elevation and dictates a downward thrust before forward movement can be obtained.

Foot spacing is an individual matter. The best results in the start are obtained through a constant search for the position which permits the back to remain parallel to the ground. As indicated in the angles, the leg should be positioned to encourage an initial forward thrust which will permit the feet to act in a well-coordinated power thrust from the blocks.

There must be firm pressure against the blocks in preparation for the thrust. The foot spacing must be only as far apart as adherence to the angle principles will permit. The firm even pressure of the feet will encourage a pushing action which will be described in this chapter.

On-the-Mark Position

The position of the hands, arms, the back, feet and body angle have been described above.

The arms should be straight under the shoulders and not with the elbows locked. Do not overemphasize tension upon the arms because it is impossible to lift the hands in an uppercut thrust to achieve the angle mentioned in No. 4 above without first unlocking the elbows. Even this small delay may affect the harmony between arms and legs which is so important in the subsequent phases of the start.

In training Lee Calhoun, 110-meter high hurdles Olympic Champion in 1956 and 1960; Vance Robinson, sprinter on the 1959 USA versus Russia and the Pan American Squads; Ed Roberts, bronze medal winner in the 200 meters in the Tokyo Olympic Games; Larry Black, silver medalist in the 1972 Olympic Games in Munich; and Charles Foster, who was ranked number one in the world in the 110-meter hurdles in 1974, it was considered helpful in all these cases to shift the weight forward to the desired pressure on the hand while still in the on-the-mark position. These sprinters felt that this would permit a con-

centration on the hip elevation and on putting proper pressure against the blocks in the next sequence of the start. Furthermore, if any adjustment of pressure should be felt necessary the sprinter can make this adjustment without affecting other phases of the start.

Get-Set Position

If proper consideration has been given to the techniques of the on-the-mark position, the hands, arms, and head will continue to remain in the correct position. However, some special attention must be given to the feet in the transition from on-the-mark to the set position. The heel-toe alignment in the two positions is not the same.

As a sprinter rises to the set position the heel must be slightly rolled back so that firm pressure can be exerted against the blocks. The sprinter must conscientiously stay back upon the blocks. The sprinter should not go too far forward in an exaggerated lean which will adversely affect the angles described between the lower leg and thigh of both legs. This common fault not only affects hip elevation but considerably reduces the explosion from the blocks that must be expected. In practice the sprinter should hold the set position while checking the details of body alignment and the angles described. This procedure will tend to make the sprinter aware of the ability to maintain a comfortable position whenever the starter holds the set position a second or two longer than usual.

A word of caution: there is a distinct difference between comfort and relaxation. The sprinter must be ready to uncoil at the sound of the gun. This action is not possible with a "relaxed sprinter."

At gun explode from blocks. The head level, directly in front of the shoulder.

As momentum is generated in the initial drive. Raising the head too quickly (looking down track to finish line) will spell disaster.

Do not develop an artificial head down position in the initial stride.

Once you have achieved the necessary drive and reached the most effective "lift point" there is no further need to keep the head down.

Initial Drive from the Blocks

The sprinter must be concerned about the first five strides. The importance of the pickup, of harmony between legs and arms, and of relaxed stride throughout the race is a known fact. To assure maximum efficiency in these phases, the sprinter must demonstrate classic form in the initial drive from the blocks.

A coordinated action between arms and legs must be developed. The "step through the hoop" action is not desirable. The sprinter must make an uppercut thrust of the arms as he/she leaves the blocks.

The head should be kept level, directly in front of the shoulder, as momentum is generated in the initial drive. Raising the head too quickly (looking down the track to the finish line) will spell disaster. The sprinter must "run up" to the best striding position. Do not develop an artificial head down position in the initial stride beyond the point of no return. Once the sprinter has achieved the necessary drive and reached the most effective "lift point" there is no further need to keep the head down. The sprinter should not be expected to stay over the knees and avoid a good knee lift by doing so.

The exact distance from the block or the exact number of strides in which the desired body lean for efficient running action will be achieved must be individually determined. Somewhere between the extremes of jerky, upward snap of the head and shoulders and an exaggerated body lean lies the point which is a happy medium.

To secure an appropriate means the runner should stand erect, then shift his weight forward until plantar flexion of the foot is required to prevent the heels from raising from the track. This position allows sufficient body lean and will provide the proper tilt forward which will tend to minimize upward bounding in the stride. Relaxed, efficient striding is the key to effective sprinting.

Striding Action

Coordinated action between legs and arms in the first few strides after start has already been described. The strides begin to lengthen as the sprinter moves into the natural running position. This stride has some distinct characteristics.

The propelling force in sprinting comes from the thrust action of the power leg (rear leg). The foot of the power leg moves downward and backward in a pushing action against the track. This delivers the thrust and permits the foot to undertake a forceful, backward sweep as a part of the entire power leg action which propels the body forward. There should be a full extension of the leg in a continued drive of the toe against the track. Premature transfer of the power leg into the recovery phase of the stride before every ounce of power has been utilized leads to a gradual loss of speed and momentum. As the leg completes its action, the knee is flexed and the leg is swung forward with the heel of the foot carried high under the buttocks.

The front leg or free-swimging leg is in the recovery stage while the power leg is in action and preparation for its transfer to the thrusting

action against the track. As the body is propelled forward, the foot of the recovery leg is moved slightly forward and should strike the ground directly under the center of gravity. There is a brief time when both feet are off the ground in efficient sprinting. Drive with the power leg in the recovery action of the free leg must be accomplished with efficiency and maximum relaxation. The forward body lean must not be exaggerated. This prevents the proper knee lift, tends to shorten the stride, and causes an unnecessary backward sweep after the thrust of the power leg.

SECTION
II

Relay Racing

RELAY RACING

Develop an Appropriate Philosophy

"Relay racing is not merely four runners participating in a baton-passing event. A relay is much more than the sum of all its parts. It is a distinct event demanding an appropriate philosophy and requiring attention to precise coaching techniques.

"It is essential for the coach and the relay participants to develop a positive, aggressive attitude toward relay racing. They must feel that an aggressive high speed pass can be successfully executed free of error within the passing zone. A cautious, restrained approach in executing the pass will usually bear bitter fruits."*

It is essential to give daily attention to details. There are 24 potential errors which can be made by the four runners in six phases of the relay legs:

1. Start and acceleration.
2. Stride transition.
3. Finish.
4. Border positions.
5. Hand-eye coordination.
6. Zone awareness.

*L.T. Walker, **Championship Techniques in Track and Field**

Hand Positions

The hand positions should be determined by baton handling variations (whether or not the baton will be exchanged from one hand to another). There are a number of factors which tend to influence whether the palm-up or palm-down method is utilized.

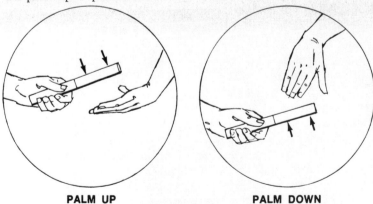

PALM UP   **PALM DOWN**

In the sprint relay pass the runners may use a palm-up or a palm-down position. The two factors which will determine the preferred hand position are: (1) the border of the lane along which the coach prefers to have the sprinter run and (2) whether or not the number two and three runners are to transfer the baton from one hand to the other during the course of the run. The rationale for having the runners negotiate the turns along the inside border is obvious. A review of the lane staggers will quickly reveal the logic in having the sprinters run the shortest possible arc. In the 400-meter relay which is run around two turns, the number one and three runners are usually considered to be the curve runners. It is important to keep the baton exchange as simple as possible. The basic goal in baton passing is to achieve a smooth exchange at maximum control speed. Complete integration of the two runners in the zone is of paramount importance. The arm-hand position is an influencing factor in this integration. The distance run on the curve will be influenced by the hand assignment.

Several options are open in executing the pass on the turn. In Option A the four competitors hold the lane border which they assume at the beginning of their relay leg. Competitors one and three run along the inside border and competitors two and four run along the outside border. The number one sprinter, the lead-off runner, starts with the baton in the right hand and passes from right to left. The other passes will be dictated by this initial start and will be left to right and right to left. This option is employed so that no transfer of the baton is required in order to make the next handoff. This option is preferred. The sprinter should practice to master these passes.

Option B — transfer of the baton. The four sprinters run the inside border. The number two and three runners shift to the inside border fifteen to twenty meters beyond the passing zone. The hand transfer is made immediately after the baton has been received and is under complete control. This option is employed as the baton is passed from right to left between all runners and at each zone.

Relay Techniques
Four additional essential components of sprint relay racing are:
1. Responsibilities of the outgoing runner.
2. Responsibilities of the incoming runner.
3. Preparing and utilizing check marks.
4. Placing the personnel.

The importance of these four components varies in accordance with the classification choice of baton exchange. In the sprint relays these four components are of nearly equal importance. In relays which demand exchanges in which there is a step up or step down of speed the coaching demands vary.

Effective passing of the baton through efficient body handling in the zones may reduce the cumulative time of a relay team by as much as 1.5 seconds. Frequently, because of four baton exchanges, runners on a relay team do not match their open race time. There is obviously a premium on coordinating the efforts of the incoming and outgoing runners.

Responsibility of the Incoming Runner

The baton is held by the rear half. All of the rear half is used to assure a firm, relaxed grip. Except at the moment of the pass in the critical passing zone, the baton is carried as an extension of the arm and hand in a series of synchronized thrusts and recoveries. No peculiar, attention-getting action should be practiced.

The baton is passed with a quick, flowing, gentle motion after the recovery of the arm immediately preceding the pass. The passing action varies according to the hand position of the outgoing runner. In the palm-down pass the form is partially extended (lowered) at the end of a recovery and the wrist is extended in order to point the baton toward the track to guarantee that it will be below the hand of the receiver. The baton is placed in the passing position only at the moment of the exchange to prevent speed-reducing, static position of the passing arm. In the palm-up pass the baton is pressed into the palm of the outgoing runner with a downward action from the thrust position. The front half of the baton is placed in the palm of the outgoing runner with a continuous press. A straight, jabbing motion of the baton is undesirable. It should be brought down to the palm of the outgoing runner with a form slightly flexed. Other factors of mechanics are essentially the same as in the palm-down pass. Coordinated practice between the incoming and outgoing runners is essential to making a successful pass.

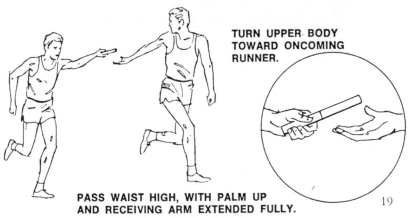

TURN UPPER BODY TOWARD ONCOMING RUNNER.

PASS WAIST HIGH, WITH PALM UP AND RECEIVING ARM EXTENDED FULLY.

19

The incoming runner and the outgoing teammate should run on separate borders of the lane if the width will permit, not even the shoulder of the two runners should overlap except in the right to right or left to left hand options. Even the slightest overlap will require the incoming runners to pass the baton across the body in order to reach the extended hand of the teammate. This position is mechanically less efficient and reduces the reach. Furthermore, the inevitable emergency arm thrust which the runner must make to effect a last ditch handoff before passing out of the zone is shortened.

The type of baton exchange determines whether the runner continues along the same border of the lane or crosses over during the race. If no hand shift is required, the outgoing runners in the second and third positions run the same border of the lane after the baton exchange is made. Should the exchange demand a change of borders, the crossover should be accomplished immediately following the completion of the pass and after the baton is under control. The sprinters running the first and fourth legs should run the appropriate border throughout their portion of the relay.

Hand-eye coordination is important. The eyes of the incoming runner should be focused on the fixed, stationary hand of the outgoing runner. The baton should be passed after there has been a focus on the hand. The incoming runner looks at the hand, not through it. The hand-eye focus begins two strides before the critical zone pass is reached and continues until the pass has been completed.

Responsibility of the Outgoing Runner

The outgoing runner must generate almost the same momentum and speed without blocks and from a crouch start as is expected when the runner uses blocks. The speed generated in the first twenty-five meters of the race is paramount. The sprinters should approximate the best time achieved over twenty-five meters in an open dash.

The best start for speed, power and momentum is from a crouch position similar to the get-set position used at the beginning of a dash. The feel of this position may be gained by:

1. Getting into the on-the-mark position with an elongated foot spread.
2. Rising to the get-set position.
3. Adjusting body weight so that the hands may be lifted from the track and adjusting foot spacing for comfort and balance.
4. Looking to the rear around the shoulder of the arm which will be extended to receive the baton. Repeating look around the shoulder of the arm which will be extended to receive the baton.

5. Practicing starts through the zone from the adjusted position, the position which permits a quick start without adjusting the feet. If the baton is to be received in the right hand, the right leg should be the dominant leg.

The outgoing runner must take literally hundreds of runs from the rear border of the zone, dropping the hand in position by simply extending the lower arm as the critical zone is reached and keeping the hand perfectly still so that the incoming runner can sight the touch position.

The Critical Passing Zone

The critical passing zone is the area in the zone where the exchange of the baton should be made. It serves as a guideline for both the incoming and the outgoing runners. The critical zone — between C and D in the diagram — is sighted by the teammates and no verbal exchange is required. More experienced runners may use verbal commands — my preference is the visual technique.

The outgoing runner has approximately twenty-two meters between point "A" (his/her starting position behind the beginning of the zone) and the beginning of the critical zone in which to generate the speed essential for an aggressive, fast, smooth pass.

Each practice sprint through the zone should include proper placement of the hands two strides before the outgoing runner reaches point "C" at the beginning of the critical zone. The incoming runner must sight the hand before the pass is attempted. It is absolutely essential that the incoming runner has an opportunity to focus on the hand target before the teammate reaches the handoff point. Proper hand coordination and timing of the pass is dependent upon three important facets of the exchange which the coach must closely observe near the critical zone: (1) the hand should be steady and in focus two strides before

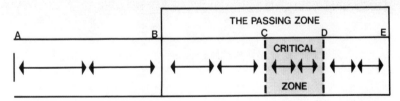

A — Hash mark in front of which runner stands.
B — Beginning of zone.
C — Beginning of critical zone.
D — End of critical zone.
E — End of zone.

the critical zone, (2) the arm extension to the rear should be at its maximum without being rigid and should not result from a backward reach, and (3) the runner should not decelerate as the arm and the hand are placed in position for the pass.

Acceleration Through the Zone

The efficiency of the outgoing runner in moving through the zone is of paramount importance. The head must remain level as the runner looks around instead of over the shoulder to sight the check mark. The hips must remain in a straight line with the head. The hips and feet are positioned for the first move down the lane and should be squared in the lane for an initial forward thrust. The "look around" must be accomplished skillfully so that the alignment of the body is not materially affected. The head must turn, not the entire body, and should be turned to face the side of the border on which the incoming runner will be traveling.

The practice sprint through the zone should start when the teammate steps into the check mark zone. The runner should be timed to determine whether the best time in an open race for the first twenty meters is being approximated.

When the proper set position is assumed, most of the weight should be on the front foot. This position will reduce the possibility of a costly slip of the foot which is certain to affect the timing. It is desirable to initiate the drive with the front foot which is steadied by the pressure placed on it from the lean position. The rear foot is brought forward sharply and close to the ground to accommodate the fast forward thrust and to maintain balance.

Effective starting through the zone is actually executed on the three commands which would normally be given in an open race — take your mark, get set, and the gun. In relay racing all three of the commands are visual. The outgoing runner goes to his mark, the appropriate position in the zone when the incoming runner is about to make his move toward the zone. The runner gets set in a crouch position when the teammate is approximately thirty meters from the check mark. The check mark is the outgoing runner's go indicator and serves the same purpose as the sound from the starter's gun. The outgoing runner executes a sprint start when the incoming runner touches the check mark area. There should be no anticipation of this touch. The mark must be touched or the plan of the check mark broken.

Handling The Baton

The baton is handed to the outgoing runner; the runner does not reach for it nor look back once the sprint has been started. There may be some variations of this in the 800-meter relay in which the outgoing runner may take a quick backward glance around the shoulder at the exchange point. The outgoing runner concentrates on placing the hand in the proper position for the baton to be pressed into the palm. The receiving hand is somewhat cupped with the fingers slightly flexed and the thumb in an extended position in order to provide the widest possible target and in order to make a quick, smooth grasp. The hand position is the same as it would be if the baton were being picked up from the track.

It is essential that the receiving hand be a steady target for the incoming runner. The outgoing runner should do a series of thrust recoveries and hand placements as a part of inplace running action so that the feel of a steady receiving hand can be felt while the body is in action. The free arm continues the pumping action as it would in

EXTEND ARMS FULLY FOR EXCHANGE. FORWARD RUNNER LOOKS STRAIGHT AHEAD, NOT BACK.

a regular running form. The runner's receiving arm should not be rigid nor pulled in toward the body. It should be in a normal extended position. The correct position of the arm on the receiving side is assumed by extending the lower arm at the elbow upon the completion of the recovery phase in the arm-thrusting action. The action is completed at the elbow, not at the shoulder. This type of arm extension reduces the error created by frequent variation of the arm and hand position when the runner reaches with the shoulder hyperextension.

Preparing and Utilizing The Check Marks

The outgoing runner must select a point behind the rear border of the zone which will serve as a handicap line for the incoming runner. If this handicap is accurately determined and there is no anticipation by the outgoing runner of his teammate striking the checkmarks, both runners should arrive at the critical zone approximately one meter apart with both traveling at nearly top speed.

Placement of the handicap mark will be determined by the speed of the incoming runner and the starting ability of the outgoing teammate. A final decision in this matter can be arrived at only through trial and error. The outgoing runner may start with eighteen to twenty feet as a point behind his standing position and increase or decrease the distance depending upon the two previously mentioned factors. The final decisions can be reached only after practicing the exchange at full speed. The distance of the handicap mark from the rear border is increased or decreased in a relationship to the point before or after the pass or point where the contact is made. The handicap mark should not be changed if either runner demonstrates a faulty movement. The runners should not attempt to adjust their speed in order to make the pass work. The changes should be made in the handicapping. Each runner should keep all factors of the pass consistent as the check mark is adjusted.

A word of caution. Once the check marks have been established, continuous practice of passing techniques may be achieved by employing 35-meter, full-speed approach runs. A shorter approach run permits many more passes and requires shorter periods of rest between baton practice sessions.

800-Meter Relay

The 800-meter relay is not merely a race twice the length of the 400-meter relay. Basically, the points discussed in the previous section on the 400-meter relay are relevant to coaching the 800-meter relay, however, some important adjustments are usually required. At least three factors influence the techniques: (1) the influencing factors of the sprinter's sustaining power in the 200-meter dash, (2) the influencing factor of wind currents at the beginning and end of the 200-meter dash, and (3) the influencing factor of diminished speed at the exchange zones due to the lift of the sprint.

The over all strength of the team may be achieved having the strong 200-meter dash man run six to eight meters longer in the race than the weaker finishers. The weaker finishers can run six to eight meters shorter by adjusting the position of the handoff in the critical zone. This can be achieved by changing check mark positions and handoff positions. For example: the position of the outgoing runner may be moved forward away from the position that would normally be assumed in the 400-meter relay. The less strong of the 200-meter runners may take the baton farther down in the zone and may pass the baton immediately upon entering the next zone.

Frequently, a runner may begin the relay with a favoring wind on one straightaway but must complete the race against a strong head wind in the opposite straightaway. This condition demands a special effort by the incoming runner to increase his body lean and to drive vigorously against the wind through the entire zone.

A windy day, and in some instances a muddy or heavy track on a non-synthetic surface, may make it necessary for the outgoing runner to decrease the initial drive away from the zone. When the wind or the track tend to slow the exchange, it is highly recommended that the semi-visual pass be utilized to guarantee a successful pass in the 800-meter relay. However, a word of caution, the semi-visual principle is applied only at the critical zone as the runner looks around the shoulder to check the incoming teammate.

Four by Four Hundred Relay

First of all the pass in the 4 x 400 relay is usually visual and frequently the palm of the outgoing runner is turned upward. Three exchanges in this relay present some challenges not found in the 4 x 100 and the 4 x 200 relays.

The most efficient and also the safest 4 x 400 baton exchange is the visual pass. The receiver stands just within the exchange zone poised to start reasonably fast as soon as the incoming runner passes a predetermined check mark which is usually from three to four meters before the exchange zone. This check mark has to be carefully judged and depends on factors that have occurred during the body of the teammates' run. It is important, however, for the outgoing runner to have some momentum as the midpoint of the zone is crossed and the baton is passed. The coach should frequently time the first hundred meters of the run to determine if between 0.3 and 0.7 of a second are being saved by the running start. This procedure is necessary to determine if the running start is contributing to a faster time. Frequently, because of faulty passing, the runner's relay time is slower than the open time when blocks are used in the 400-meter dash.

It is a responsibility of the incoming runner to get the baton into the hand of the outgoing runner. The outgoing runner should never grab for the baton but should hold the receiving hand as steady as possible until the baton is placed in it. It is very difficult to pass the baton into a hand that is grasping for it. The outgoing runner should lock the baton into the hand. The responsibility of the pass rests largely with the outgoing runner, who is fresh. The outgoing runner must move through the zone with measured, controlled speed and then quickly accelerate after the pass has been completed.

SECTION
III

The Hurdles

Hurdles

"The hurdling style should be consistent with the basic components of the body. Whether the prospective hurdler has long legs, is of average height with legs of medium length, short and exceptionally fast, or possesses some combination of these physical attributes, these characteristics as well as limitations of hip mobility, suppleness, speed and like qualities should be the qualities which determine hurdle clearance pattern and stride form."[*]

The hurdles is a sprint event. Unlike the flat sprint event in which both the option of increasing frequency of stride and length of stride are open to the sprinter, only improved frequency is a viable option to the hurdler. Therefore, the problem facing the hurdler is to minimize raising the center of mass at clearance, keep hurdle clearance time to a minimum and assume sprint form at the earliest possible moment. The hurdler is a sprinter with ten or less interruptions.

How to achieve the most efficient sprint form after the interruption at the barrier is of prime importance. Two overall factors influence the return to sprint action.

1. Maintenance of horizontal velocity in clearance.
2. Effective coordination of arms and legs.

THE START
Approach to First Hurdle and Takeoff

An essential to the sprint start described in the chapter on Sprinting applies to the start of the hurdle race. One important additional consideration in the hurdles' start is the influence that foot placement in the blocks has upon the determination of the lead leg and the trail leg.

The hurdler should use a style of starting and running which will enable the hurdler to bring the body up to sprinting angle or full running position at least by the end of the fourth stride. Effective clearance of a barrier fifteen yards from the starting line demands a smooth, settled running action in the last three or four strides. Any adjustment in the stride pattern after the fourth stride will prove costly.

[*]L.T. Walker, **Championship Techniques in Track and Field**

The lead leg preference for the straightaway hurdle race is the left leg. The left leg will provide an advantage for the hurdler if it is necessary to run a hurdles race around a curve. However, the coach should accept the lead leg preference of the hurdler in terms of which leg is instinctively thrown over the hurdle in a simple running drill. In order to get the hurdler in position for takeoff at the first hurdle in the desired number of strides, the coach can adjust the position of the feet in the blocks to assure an even number or an odd number of strides to the first hurdle. If the hurdler arrives at the takeoff position for the first hurdle at maximum control speed in eight strides, his lead leg should be placed in the rear block. A hurdler with a long, fast stride may use seven strides and, therefore, should put the lead leg foot in the front block.

Once the approach run to the first hurdle has been selected, the exact length of each of the first three strides should be measured and recorded. Practice to the first hurdle should be repeated over and over again until the stride plan is fixed and remains constant. The hurdler should not vary the stride lengths even when practicing with sprinters without hurdles. The emphasis should be on improving stride frequency or speed of leg reflex within the theme stride length plan. If in earlier practice sessions the takeoff or hurdle clearance does not come out right within the selected stride plan, the adjustment in stride length should be made in the first three strides. Should the athlete, early in the season, experience difficulty in reaching the first hurdle, it may be placed some few inches nearer the starting line in order to prevent overstretching to clear it. Once confidence is established and speed of leg reflex and stride length pattern have been established, the hurdle can be placed back in its normal position.

Maintenance of Velocity

Up to the moment of takeoff, all aspects of sprint start acceleration apply to the hurdler. The horizontal velocity established must be

maintained by minimizing elevation of center of mass through effective body lean and lowered head position. Do not jump up. Remain in an attacking position.

It is essential to drive into the hurdle with a stepover action. A synchronized trunk lean with the lead leg trends to reduce the amount of vertical movement which contributes to a longer time in the air and, therefore, a slower hurdle clearance. The trunk lean also places the body in a better position for action and reaction of the lead arm and trail leg. Although the hurdler's eyes are focused ahead at the moment of clearance, the head should stay lowered so that the center of mass can remain low. The important thing to remember is that the hurdler should be comfortably settled into the proper running action during the first hurdle. Control speed is usually about seven-eights of the runner's maximum speed. This should get the runner to the first hurdle between 2.1 and 2.5 seconds for the good to fair hurdler, respectively.

Takeoff is from the ball of the foot as in a regular running stride. The heel must not be planted. The rear foot delivers explosive power for the drive from the track. The hips are driven upward and forward to produce a dive for the hurdle and a step-over action rather than a jump-over action. As the hurdler rises to the hurdle, the lead leg motion is with the knee. The knee is raised as in a regular running stride and the foot of the lead leg is lifted as high as a synchronized body dip will permit.

A word of caution: if in the reach for the hurdle the lead foot is a little more forward and the lead leg is slightly straighter than is recommended by theory, do not become alarmed if the straight leg does not produce kicking action toward the top rail of the hurdle. Some of the very best hurdlers in the world have had a slightly straight lead leg.

The rush of the lead leg may be an adjustment for the slightly advanced action of the trail leg to ensure balance for the scissor action of the leg. Experience has proven that if the straight leg does not cur-

tail effective clearance and permits the speedy leg action over the hurdle which is essential for a rapid clearance, the hurdler does not have to worry about the position of the slightly straight lead leg. However, if the young hurdler locks the lead leg and tends to sail out before the lead leg can be brought down toward the track, the coach may teach a slightly higher knee lift with the leg in a very slight flexion in preparation for the snapdown.

As the lead foot reaches its highest point and begins its downward action to the track, there is a reach forward with the trail knee. The trail leg should not be hurried across the barrier; instead, the foot should deliver every ounce of power by its thrust against the track. The trail leg is lifted and pulled through by hip action. The greatest pull is exerted when the knee of the trail leg is about fifteen inches from the top of the hurdle. This action is a very vigorous hip circle.

If, contrary to generally accepted theory, the hurdler tends to make a premature forward rush of the trail leg to get the knee "cocked" for quick movement across the hurdle, check the driving force toward the hurdle and the head elevation to determine whether there is a jumping-up action. Let hurdle clearance time determine whether it is a major error. If the hurdler has delivered full power (not an overextended ham string) and the trail leg knee remains behind the bar to be whipped through with a synchronized chopping-down action of the lead leg, do not be rushed into altering the style.

If the action is continuous and there is no hanging of the trail leg which will require a two-part action, a slightly early lift of the foot from the track may not be harmful. The foot of the trail leg should be everted as the thigh rises and the rear knee is brought through into forward line under the breast for the next stride.

The Synchronized Arm Action

Remember that in hurdling the arms are utilized to help maintain balance. There is no standardized arm action for all hurdlers. The key to the correct use of the arms is whether they permit the shoulder to remain square, tend to give the hurdler greater balance in landing, and can quickly flow into the normal sprinting action. If the hurdler achieves this but makes an arm movement slightly contrary to the accepted theory, there should be no attempt to change the arm action. A desirable practice in effective clearance is to drive the lead arm slightly across the body. This placement permits a greater arc in the fast recovery of the lead arm, thereby minimizing rotary action and preventing an off-balance landing. A word of caution: the sweeping arc should draw the shoulder out of the squared position to the finish line.

It should be repeated here that the hurdler may feel more at ease if both arms start forward together. The arm opposite the lead leg continues shooting forward slightly ahead of the opposite arm to help keep the hurdler square and balanced.

It is recommended in teaching young hurdlers proper clearance to use a canvas top as a replacement for the usual barrier. As the hurdler builds confidence for sharp, precise clearance after many hours of practice the canvas may be replaced. Nothing will bring a high sail any quicker than a few bruised knees and ankles brought about as the coach tries to reduce clearance time.

Transition from Hurdle Clearance to Sprint Action

The hurdler's upper body should land in a sprinter's position over the foot of the lead leg approximately four feet from the hurdle (depending upon hurdling style). The recovery of the lead arm is made with the elbow and should come back just high enough to clear the trail knee. The action of the trail leg will influence the stride pattern between hurdles. The distance traveled in the air will determine the distance the hurdler must cover in the three strides between the hurdles. This distance is usually about nineteen feet.

It should be emphasized that upon landing the hurdler becomes a sprinter in the strides between the hurdles. All practice should be directed at the simple procedure of developing the fastest possible sprint.

A sluggish trail leg will delay the start of the sprint. A trail leg which is thrust to the ground prematurely will shorten the first stride after landing and therefore affect the sprint action between hurdles. This action will demand an overstriding in one or both of the remaining two strides.

Hurdling Positions

There are four positions from which the coach should view the hurdler during practice sessions: (1) front view, (2) side view nearest the lead leg, (3) side view nearest the trail leg, and (4) the rear view. I would like to discuss some points which may be observed from two views — the front and side view composite.

Front View

There are many facets of the correct hurdling form which are important. Among these are (1) shoulder position, (2) lead leg foot action, and (3) eye focus.

Shoulder Position — Shoulder rotated away from the squared position (also observed from the side view). This is one of the most serious deficiencies because of the torsion action it induces. The young hurdler frequently places himself/herself in an unfavorable position by initiating the recovery of the lead arm at the shoulder. A forceful thrust moves the shoulder away from the squared position and often induces a circular uppercut action in attempting to achieve the necessary thrust position prior to the next arm extension.

The corrective action suggested for this deficiency is to utilize the opening-door action from the elbow. The action is initiated at the elbow in order to get the extended arm back to the thrust position. Simply flex at elbow.

Lead Leg Action — Check the action of the lead leg. The action should be straight over the hurdle and not a circular motion. Circular motion is usually caused by "toeing in" or crowding the hurdle at takeoff. The former is corrected by working on the "toeing out" position, the latter by moving the takeoff spot back to a normal position of approximately 6½ feet.

Toeing In Circular Action And Opening Trail Leg Correction

1. Wall drill — place a line on wall 42 inches from the floor. Mark spots on the floor directly in front of line on the wall. One line should be 5' from wall, the other 6' from the wall. The hurdler should begin by standing at the 5' distance and extending his leg in hurdling fashion to strike the wall. Both the foot of the lead leg and the foot of the trail leg should be pointed straight at the wall. When the hurdler achieves the correct position at the 5' distance, move him back to 6 or 6½'.
2. Running in place — the hurdler runs in place in front of a hurdle or in the drill listed above. Use a step-over type action to extend the lower leg toward the hurdle or wall. CAUTION: DO

NOT PERMIT EXTENSION TO BE MADE FROM HIP.
3. Hip circles exercises:
   a. Weight training to strengthen ilio-psoas group (groin muscle).
   b. Place 4 hurdles 7 feet apart. Do trail leg exercises. As the drill is mastered, decrease spacing between hurdles to 6 feet. The trail leg must be quickly brought up from track over each hurdle as the lead leg is kept outside of the hurdle. The knee should be pointed toward the next hurdle as the toe of the trail leg foot remains everted.

Eye Focus — Concentration on hurdle in advance of clearance to prevent head drop.

Side View

The side view is taken from two or more angles. The coach should observe a number of procedures which may be followed in correcting hurdling errors. Among these are:
1. Check takeoff spot.
   a. Measure the distance between spike marks of takeoff foot and hurdle. (Place tape on all-weather tracks at desired distance from hurdle. Check spike marks in relation to tape.) If takeoff at first hurdle is too close, causing a circular motion of lead leg, shorten one or more of the strides between the hurdles. Do not over-reach in the stride before takeoff.
2. The lead leg action and body lean should be a single coordinated act. Do not make it a two-piece action.
   a. Lead leg action over hurdle continues as a part of a normal stride. The thigh is parallel to the ground before the lower leg is extended. **Action does not begin from the track.**
   b. The hurdler should practice extending the lead leg against a gymnasium wall with simultaneous dip from waist to get chin close to knee.
3. Check for a premature lift of the trail leg foot from track. This action causes loss of momentum and often results in sitting on top of hurdle.
   a. Place a mark 5 to 6 feet from wall. Drive the lead leg to wall with takeoff foot remaining in contact with floor. Takeoff leg should be fully extended. **Watch for hyperextension.**
   b. Strengthen hip circle muscles to assure a continuous, coordinated pull and snapthrough of trail leg from takeoff through first stride.
4. Leg-reflex speed drills.
   a. Lead leg only over hurdles.

b. Trail leg only over hurdles.

c. 5 step drill between hurdles at regular distance.

d. 4 hurdles trail leg drill with hurdles 7 feet apart.

5. Use of watch. Time over 1, 5, 8, 12.

1	2	3 to 5	6 to 8	9 to 10
2.5	1.4	1.3	1.2	1.3
2.8				

To improve total hurdling time, the speed must be improved in one or more of the above segments.

Intermediate Hurdles

The basic qualifications of the high hurdler are almost as important to the intermediate hurdler. In addition courage, endurance, and control are essential.

There are several basic points which should be considered in training for the intermediate hurdles.

1. The longer approach run to the first hurdle (49.21 yards or 45 meters) will demand strict attention to the dimensions of frequency and length of stride.
2. Left lead leg is preferred because of the need to run on a curve. However, it is important but not an absolute necessity as some coaches may believe.
3. The degree of trunk lean is slightly less than in the high hurdles. It is not necessary to have as pronounced a layout over the hurdles since the hurdle is lower than in the high hurdles. It is easier to negotiate and emphasis should be made on maintaining forward lean off the hurdle as well as into it.
4. Arm action and the position of the head are the same as in the high hurdles, possibly with the exception of those using the double arm thrust.
5. The lead leg action is essentially the same. However, intermediate hurdlers with short legs may find it to their advantage to sail the barrier before the snapdown in order to get closer to the next hurdle.
6. The trail leg is delayed slightly then pulled through quickly with the action being similar to that in the high hurdles. The knee can be brought through flatter but the hurdler must step out with the trail leg in order to be moving closer to and in the direction of the next hurdle.
7. Approximately 103 feet running distance between hurdles after clearance can be covered in varying stride plans. The most effec-

tive plan among the best hurdlers is the stride plan with fifteen strides between hurdles. The taller, more mature hurdlers find that thirteen strides are more effective, while younger hurdlers may find it necessary to use seventeen strides. As the hurdler gains confidence, strength, and endurance, other patterns will be available to him. Some of the patterns are listed below.

a. 15 to 17-stride plan in which the hurdler changes from 17 to 15 at some point in the race. The stronger hurdlers may make these changes much further into the race plan.

b. 15 strides all the way.

c. 13-15 strides with the hurdler changing at some point in the race from 15 to 13 strides, depending upon the conditions of the race.

d. 13 strides all the way for the more advanced hurdlers.

e 14 strides which demands alternating lead legs. In the 14-stride plan the coach must develop a set of drills that will assist the hurdler in taking the hurdle with a right lead leg smoothly and with good balance. Failing to do this will eliminate all of the advantage that can be gained by running aggressively at the hurdle in 14 strides. It should be noted here that as a rule of thumb the 14-stride combination is usually followed by the advanced hurdler who has used 13 strides in the early part of the race. This transition precludes having to use both legs throughout the body of the race, a most difficult feat.

Speed and rhythm between hurdles should be consistent but may be influenced by elements of the weather and the conditions of the running surface. It is absolutely essential in the intermediate hurdles for the hurdler to be timed to the first hurdle and also times established between hurdles. The coach can then determine which segment of the race is being adversely affected. A sample of some complete hurdle splits are listed below. The second series of splits represents the time of a world record holder, Ed Moses, 1976 Olympic Champion and 1979 and 1981 World Cup Champion.

Splits Intervals

	1	2	3	4	5	6	7	8	9	10	Finish
Elapsed Time	6.3	10.4	14.6	18.8	23.0	27.6	32.2	36.8	41.4	46.0	51.6
Each Hurdle	6.3	4.1	4.2	4.2	4.2	4.6	4.6	4.6	4.6	4.6	5.6

Ed Moses

1	2	3	4	5	6	7	8	9	10	Finish
5.9	9.8	13.7	17.5	21.4	25.5	29.8	34.1	38.4	42.7	47.8
5.9	3.9	3.9	3.8	3.9	4.1	4.3	4.3	4.3	4.3	5.1

The training format outline in the chapter on sprinting for the long sprinter is appropriate in training the intermediate hurdler. The cycle plan with pole progressions and regressions and the program of split 300 and 500 are excellent drills to develop the endurance that is essential to run the intermediate hurdles. Stride plan adjustments should be selected on the basis of the height and leg length of the hurdler rather than the hurdler's inability to continue a selected plan because of lack of endurance and strength. The training format should be designed to develop those factors so that the hurdler's attention can be given to the development of proper techniques.

SECTION
IV

Distance Running

DISTANCE RUNNING

Middle distance and distance running are closely associated in form, technique and training methods. There are, however, some important variations which should be noted. The techniques for developing distance runners differ with coaches throughout the U.S. and the world. In spite of the variations in training methods, there is considerable agreement in five essential aspects of distance running which have contributed to recent achievements:

1. The athlete must have the physiological and psychological equipment to endure pain and fatigue.
2. The athlete must develop the discipline which permits and encourages vigorous practice.
3. The athlete must have good balance between natural speed and endurance, a quality which must be developed and attained through hard work.
4. The athlete endowed with great natural ability will need several years of conditioning to achieve great heights.
5. The athlete must develop an intelligent approach to running with sound racing tactics.

Stamina, pace, judgment, form and speed are important considerations in distance running. Training methods employed to achieve maximum results in these components have shown considerable variation. However, it is generally agreed that the training schedule is partially individual and that frequent adaptations must be made in the schedule according to individual conditions and capabilities.

Conditioning For Stamina

One of the factors which separates a Sebastian Coe, Steve Ovett, Steve Scott, John Walker, Kip Kieno, or Mirus Ifter from merely good distance runners is their ability to sustain a running form and generate speed after some long, stressful running.

Conditioning for stamina must be approached with understanding about the athlete's complete season. The planning of preliminary and early-season training schedules is influenced by a number of factors: cross country, indoor competition, beginning and closing dates of outdoor competition. These competitions revolve around local, national, and even international competition.

There are many conditioning methods which have been successfully employed by coaches and athletes. Some of the methods have been discussed in the chapter on training and have been used both singly and in combinations. When the choice of methods has been exercised it is necessary to carefully structure and supervise weight-training programs to avoid injury from overload and improper performance of movement. It is advisable to conduct an early conditioning program of beginners on the track.

Three points to be considered basic in the conditioning program that seem to be common among all the systems or methods of training are:

1. The warmup is an essential phase of the total schedule. The systems of the body must first be brought to an adjustment for strenuous exercise. The time required to accomplish this varies from athlete to athlete but 30-50 minutes is usually adequate. There are many variations employed by great distance runners but the period may be divided as follows:

easy jogging	6-10 minutes
light calisthenics	15-20 minutes
more easy jogging	3-5 minutes
easy to heavy striding	4-10 minutes
2 or 3 50-60 yard sprints	

   Warmup preceding competition should be guided by this axiom — run as hard in the last part of the warmup as would be required any time in the race. The warmup should be followed by a 12-15 minutes recovery period.

2. Strenuous work days to develop stamina should be followed by a light day's work. There are many variations of this particular point but a recommended plan in the preliminary season may be as follows:

   Monday — over distance
   Tuesday — pace running
   Wednesday — heavy work load
   Thursday — pace running
   Friday — speed
   Saturday — fartlek.

   This plan must be varied when competition begins. A rest day prior to competition is valuable, however some athletes tend to thrive on some moderate running even the day before competition.

3. The runner should leave the practice session with a feeling of exhilaration. The work load should be adjusted to complete every phase of it without falling apart. Achieving maximum load is accomplished by gradually increasing the distance of the total time of the run, reducing the length of the rest periods, or a combination of the above.

There is considerable advantage in dividing the data program into several days. Each phase of the workout should be presented to the runner as a separate segment of the day's total workout. If appropriate recovery periods are utilized, the runner will approach each new segment with enthusiasm. Mental fatigue often associated with day-long plans will be avoided. For more experienced runners whose goals are high and for whom motivation is no problem, the long range workout schedule should be posted in the log book. In order to develop the aerobic system required for distance running and to be able to engage in quality finish, the individual must be able to do quantity and quality running with great enthusiasm.

It is highly recommended that a log book be kept. The athlete and the coach can plan schedules several days ahead. The log book is a valuable reference tool because schedules often cannot be followed absolutely to the letter. It may be necessary to vary or even completely change the conditioning program because the athlete suffers from mental or physical fatigue or from severe changes in the weather.

Pace Judgment

Even though it is important to log many miles in developing stamina and endurance, the ability to know how fast to run is absolutely essential. Some distance runners learn this skill very quickly while others require a great deal of practice in order to be able to develop a sense of pace. All athletes who run middle distances and long distances must practice the art of pace judgment, a skill which must be learned in the early training season.

There are many pace schedules available to the athlete and coach. In training sessions the important thing is to develop a sense of timing so sensitive to the style of the runner that the body becomes a stop watch. The track may be divided into segments of 100s, 200s or 300s and the practice over these distances should be repeated until the athlete can master running these segments in the time which has been designated. In some instances, the segments should be run at the pace expected in the competition. In early practice sessions the coach must continuously advise the athlete of the time that is being achieved so that a consciousness of pace can be developed. If there is too much variation in the time on the slow side or the fast side, the coach should have the athlete repeat the segment until pace judgment is mastered. (Some of the workout schedules at the end of the chapter are excellent for developing pace judgment.)

Development of Speed

The distance runner does not have a native capacity for great speed.

However, the coach must be aware of the fact that some speed work is absolutely essential in order to develop this important component of the distance runner's program. This cannot be left to chance. There is a change in the use of muscles in distance running. The stride action during a distance race changes in intensity on the striding muscles. During the body of the race the runner will depend largely on the striding muscles. Near the end of a race or sometimes during trouble spots during the body of the race the runner must rely on the sprint muscles. This calls for a different body position, a different arm and leg action and a change of tempo. This must be included in the distance runner's workout.

Development of Running Form

Stride length is one of the principal variants in running techniques. One axiom holds true: the slower the run, the shorter the length of the stride; the faster the run, the longer the stride length. Because two short strides carry the runner farther than one long stride and require far less energy, the distance runner adjusts stride length as an important consideration of economy of effort. It is essential to eliminate all action that tends to impede smooth, flowing action and wastes energy.

The arm action should be natural and relaxed. An unnatural arm position leads to upper body tension and tired aching arms which affect other aspects of the running form. The arms are used for balance and to compensate for upper body torsion resulting from the striding action. As the left leg goes forward during the stride, the left shoulder tends to be pulled forward and the right shoulder and right side of the upper body move backward.

Another axiom must be remembered when discussing the position and action of the arms: the faster the run, the higher the arms are carried and the more vigorous the arm thrusts. The arm position is lowered and the arm thrust diminished as the distance of the run increases. The arms are carried fairly low in distance running (hip height) with a normal elbow bend in what is referred to as "the weight in the elbow" relaxed position.

Leg Action

Leg action is what propels the runner and is divided into three phases: (1) the driving phase, (2) the support phase, and (3) the recovery phase.

The drive phase of the stride begins when the center of gravity has passed ahead of the supporting foot which is in contact with the track. The forward drive is gained through a straight-forward pointed plant of the foot (which is more nearly flat with no heel-first breaking action). The toe leaves the track with maximum thrust at the conclusion of the stride.

The foot contacts the ground directly under the projected center of gravity. When the foot is flat on the track, it bears the runner's full weight, and the body moves forward in a smoothly executed flow in preparation for the next stride following the recovery phase of the opposite leg.

The recovery phase begins when the support leg leaves the running surface behind the body. As the foot leaves the surface, the lower leg folds up toward the thigh and the heel rises toward the hip. This action is minimized in distance running. This kick up in the recovery

helps to shorten the lever of the legs and permits the shortened leg lever to swing forward more quickly in a pendulum action for the next stride. The knee is lifted, not thrown forward, the hips remain loose.

A generalization can be made about the correct form in distance running relative to fast stride, length of stride, leg and arm action and body lean. As the distance of the run increases, the forward lean decreases, the knee lift is lessened, the length of stride decreases, the arms are lowered and thrust less vigorous, and the foot stride is nearly flat.

SECTION
V

The Horizontal Jumps

THE LONG AND TRIPLE JUMPS

The long and triple jumps are similar, yet the two are in some aspects quite different. Both have four phases: (1) the approach run, (2) the takeoff, (3) in-flight, and (4) the landing. However, the triple jump has three takeoff phases, one each in the hop, step and jump phases and also three in-flight phases.

The Approach

In both horizontal jumps, the approach run is most critical. A successful, well-executed jump cannot be done without a smooth, relaxed and controlled approach run. A good approach run involves a compromise between stride frequency and stride length.

The approach run length varies from 100 to 140 feet (with an average of about 120 feet). The length of the approach run is influenced by the basic speed and quickness of the jumper. The speed of the approach run is usually about 75-80 percent of the full speed of the jumper with a gradual acceleration from the starting checkmark. It is necessary to retain the speed until the takeoff.

Most jumpers in their speedy, relaxed, controlled approach run tend to shorten the last three strides before takeoff to avoid a stretching action for the board. The stretch action at the board will place the body weight too far behind the takeoff foot. This will tend to act as a braking force to the good forward speed and will also limit the lift from the takeoff board.

The success of the entire approach run and the success of the jumps will depend on how the approach run is initiated in the first two or three strides. The jumper must achieve consistency of length and frequency.

Determining the Check Marks

Determining the check mark to guarantee successful striking of the takeoff board requires special attention to details. One check mark at the beginning of the approach is preferred so that the jumper can concentrate on the relaxed sprint effort. To achieve the end of using only one mark, six steps should be followed in determining the start of the approach run.

1. Measure on the track the number of feet from a takeoff point which, according to the speed of the jumper, would be required for effective jumping. Mark that point on the track.
2. Beginning at the designated point, sprint with gradual acceleration toward the line which represents the takeoff board. With occasional rest periods to allow recovery time, do this approach a dozen or more times. Check each approach run for relaxation and gradual acceleration at nearly full effort.
3. Mark the strike point near the edge of the runway nearest to the takeoff line.
4. Draw a line where the cluster of marks is made. If the cluster is not in line with the board, measure the distance from the line to the imaginary line with the board.
5. Move the tentative starting check mark forward or backward the same distance measured from the cluster of marks to the takeoff board.
6. Measure the exact distance from the newly established check mark to the takeoff point. This is now the distance which should be established on the runway.
7. Check marks should be used during early development then eliminated as soon as possible so that there will not be the tendency to cue on them for the acceleration pattern.

The Takeoff

The jumper must attempt to get sufficient height at takeoff to allow time in the in-flight phase to execute leg extension. However, height alone is not enough. The action at takeoff is a forward-upward lift.

Five essential points must be emphasized in executing the takeoff:

1. The shorter last stride permits a slight bend of the takeoff leg. A powerful extension of the bent leg provides a forward-upward lift from the takeoff board.
2. The takeoff foot strikes the board ahead of the center of gravity.
3. The foot should strike the board firmly in a "flat-foot" position. In this action, the heel lands first, but there is no attempt to execute a heel ball-toe rock-up action.

4. The body weight should be directly over the board as the takeoff foot strikes it, but it should be very slightly in advance of the takeoff foot as the jumper leaves the board.
5. The final thrust into the air results from running off the board. Most good jumpers take off at an angle of not more than 25 degrees. The greater the speed at takeoff, the lesser the angle.

The jumper should stride off the board in a sprint action. The body weight must be moved slightly forward with the head high and with the eyes focused on some imaginary spot high and beyond the pit. The chest should be elevated. The knee opposite the takeoff leg is thrust forward and high as the arms move vigorously in a counterbalancing action. There should be no physical change in the jumper's sprinting pattern until the next to last stride which is slightly longer.

It is essential to work diligently to control stride length of the last two strides as described. If the last stride is too short, the center of gravity will pass too far ahead of the takeoff foot. This will reduce the lift off the board and produce excessive forward rotation. This action will prevent proper leg extension and proper landing. The contact period of the takeoff foot will be reduced and, therefore, will not allow proper execution of the takeoff.

If the last stride is too long, forward speed will be lost because the center of gravity would be over the board at the moment of takeoff. Vertical lift would be improved but the important horizontal velocity would be decreased.

Flight

The two styles most frequently used by jumpers are (1) the Hitch-kick (running in the air) and (2) the Hang.

Hitch-Kick (Running in the air)

Running in the air is a reaction fight against the downward pull of gravity. There is no gain in the momentum, but the style does reduce the difficulty of holding the legs up and helps in bringing the body to the correct position at the right time.

The running in the air technique or hitch-kick requires:

1. Driving the knee of the free leg high as the takeoff leg stretches down.
2. Stretching the free leg straight forward, down, and then bending it as it passes back under the body.
3. Snapping the takeoff leg quickly forward in the same manner as the free leg was moved in the takeoff action.
4. Bringing the heel of the leg which began the running action (free leg at takeoff) adjacent to the heel of the takeoff leg, holding the head up with eyes focused straight forward.

The arms must be kept high and moving as they do in sprinting action. The chest must be elevated. The upper body must be kept erect and the head kept high.

The Hang

The hang style is used mainly by jumpers with great lift. The hang style requires excellent timing.

The flight action in the hang is as follows:

1. The free leg is stretched forward and then dropped beneath the body.

2. The takeoff leg is thrust forward from the board to a position next to the free leg.
3. The arms drop back to the side.
4. The trunk is held erect, the head high, and the chest lifted.
5. The legs whip forward and upward in a vigorous stretching action.
6. The arms press forward and downward in the landing position.

Landing

It is important that the jumper does not bend the trunk toward the thigh until the last moment before the legs are extended for landing. When the jumper hits the pit, the chest should be thrust forward as the knees are flexed.

Immediately before contact with the landing surface, the feet must be extended as far as possible in front of the body and the sand, the arms should be pressed forward and downward.

The Triple Jump

There are some major differences between the long jump and the triple jump. In secondary schools the long jumper will usually be expected to double in the triple jump. Therefore the jumper must understand the basic differences in the performance of the long and triple jump. These differences must be carefully practiced after the approach, takeoff, flight, and landing phases of the long jump have been thoroughly learned.

The developing jumper should carefully consider seven basic differences in the technique of the long and triple jumps:

1. The body lean at takeoff is more pronounced in the triple jump. The last stride is not shortened because vertical lift is not required.
2. The takeoff (for the hop) is executed low with minimum elevation. The head up position with eyes focused forward is common to both.
3. The body position and elevation changes in each flight of the triple jump in contrast to the single flight of the long jump. The changes in the triple jump are from a very slight forward lean at takeoff in the hop to a nearly erect position in the jump. With each increase in height, careful attention must be given to sustaining the forward momentum. The landing foot is directly under the center line of the body.
4. The triple jumper must master a coordinated, synchronized bending and unbending of the knees in the three flights as compared to the single action of the long jump.
5. The distance factor in the triple jump is influenced by the execution of three distinct flights instead of one. The step flight is the one that most often requires lengthening. The complete pattern must be considered when adjusting any flight distance.

6. The stronger (best) jumping leg should be used in the third phase of the jump. Arrange the three phases to place the jumper in position for a strong final jump.
7. The triple jumper must establish a pattern of distance for each phase of the jump. The established ratio for the phases will provide a measuring rod to determine which phase is inadequate.

SECTION
VI

The Vertical Jumps

THE HIGH JUMP

The Fosbury Flop has quickly become the most popular form of high jumping and involves four major areas: (1) approach, (2) foot plant, (3) takeoff, and (4) bar clearance.

The high jump basically involves transferring horizontal velocity to vertical velocity. The essential movement is upward rather than forward. Speed and rhythm must be maintained throughout the entire technique.

The key to an effective, successful jump is how high the jumper can raise his/her center of mass. Raising the center of mass to its maximum over the bar must be an important consideration and, therefore, practice sessions must be devoted to accomplishing this end. This factor is significantly affected by the approach run, the plant and the takeoff.

The Approach

The high jumper is first a runner as the approach phase of the jump is executed. Speed is important but the acceleration must be controlled. Speed will vary among jumpers.

The approach to the high jump follows a ''J'' shaped curve involving 7-11 steps from the takeoff. Three marks should be established by the high jumper: (1) start, (2) inside mark, and (3) foot plant and takeoff.

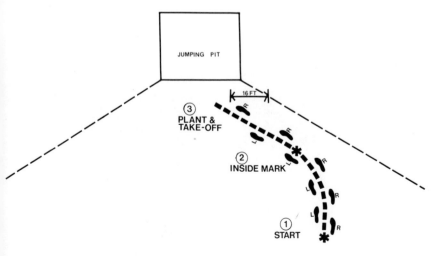

Approximately five steps from the start the jumper should lean left as curving in begins, thus bringing the jumper to a position almost parallel to the crossbar. The jumper should initiate the curve of the approach with the outside foot so that crossover steps on the curve is not necessary. The next to the last step should be long in order to lower the center of gravity, and the arms should be gathering for the double arm lift.

The next to last stride is slightly longer and influences the lowering of the hips without a leaning back. The lowering of the center of mass and the positioning of the arms away from and to the rear of the body in that next to last stride must be accomplished with minimum loss of speed. The last stride is the shortest of the last three strides and should contribute to a fast movement of the center of mass over the takeoff foot. A backward lean or a long last stride will dictate that the center of mass will move slowly in the last stride.

Foot Plant

Only one foot may be used for the flop takeoff. Most right-handed people push off with the left foot. The left foot should be planted heel first between the near pole and the middle of the bar; the foot should be pointed toward the far pole. As indicated, the high jumper must strive to elevate the center of mass into the air as high as possible. The impulse over the plant foot should be of very short duration. The quick vertical thrust accompanied by the rotational component contributes 90% to the lift factor, in relation to the height attained. It is absolutely essential that the arms are moved upward in a quick thrust as the foot is planted in preparation for the takeoff. This action provides an impulse over the plant foot of short duration.

Takeoff

The takeoff involves converting forward momentum to upward momentum. At the time of the takeoff the arms drive up to shoulder height and the bent lead knee nearest the bar drives upward until it is parallel to the ground. This raises the center of mass and rotates the body so that the back is to the bar.

The takeoff foot should be placed in front of the center of mass at approximately 20 degrees in relationship to the bar and aimed at the far standard. The knee of the free leg must be thrust upward in a quick move and decelerated when the leg is parallel to the takeoff surface (block out). The quick deceleration will help in generating additional vertical momentum.

In the "J" approach, as the jumper turns for the bar and prepares for the takeoff the eyes then pick up the bar or top of rear standard. This shift in eye focus from straight ahead will help the jumper estimate speed and time the arm action in preparation for the vertical transfer.

POLE VAULT

Pole Selection

The personal preference of the vaulter should be the guiding principle in pole selection. Selecting the vaulting pole to fit the athlete is accomplished by trial and error, in spite of the fact that manufacturers publish a guide to proper ordering. The four factors which will influence the selection of the pole are its strength, its flexibility, its elasticity, and its durability.

The pole should be selected by handhold and weight. Selecting a pole lighter than the vaulter's weight will not only hinder the performance but could become hazardous because it may break. A pole which is too soft will be bent to an extreme of more than 90 degrees and thrust the vaulter to the rear of the pit. A pole which bends too much may result in the vaulter pushing the pole against the pit, which will preclude the vaulter waiting for the pole to respond naturally and forcing him to bail out of the jump. A pole which is too stiff will throw the vaulter back on the runway without entering the landing surface.

Ordering a vaulting pole of 15 foot length for a vaulter who has a top handgrip of 13 feet will not "work" for the vaulter. It will be too stiff.

The Grip and Pole Carry

Stand the pole vertically in front of the vaulter. Have him place his right hand on the pole slightly above his head. (Figure 1)

Now have the vaulter place the tip of the pole out in front of him, bringing the right hand and pole to a resting position on the right shoulder, keeping the shoulders squared and extending the left arm down the pole to grasp it. This is his handhold. (Figure **2** & **3**)

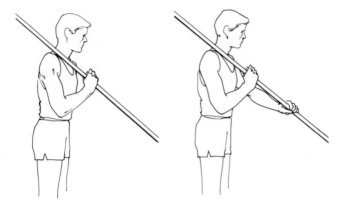

Two types of pole carry are prominent. Strong vaulters who have great speed in the approach run carry the pole horizontally to the ground and straight forward in the direction of the run.

Lighter athletes tend to carry the pole diagonally across the body with the end about head high. (Figure **5**). This carry brings the center of gravity of the pole closer to the vaulter and makes it possible to generate greater speed in the latter stage of the approach run. Each vaulter should decide on the carry best suited to his characteristics.

The Approach Run

The approach run should be long enough to allow for a relaxed start and gradual acceleration to reach maximum controlled speed at the moment of the plant. The speed on the runway and the placement of the pole will influence a dynamic takeoff and give greater energy to the pole. The length of the run varies between 98 and 145 feet, depending on the sprint ability and experience of the vaulter.

The use of check marks varies according to the ability and experience of the vaulter. Generally, two marks are used. The first mark is to indicate the starting point of the run. The beginning vaulter may utilize a check mark at the midpoint of the runway to help in the development of a rhythmic running pattern.

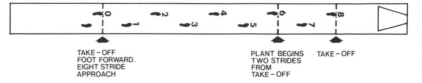

TAKE-OFF
FOOT FORWARD.
EIGHT STRIDE
APPROACH

PLANT BEGINS   TAKE-OFF
TWO STRIDES
FROM
TAKE-OFF

The vaulter may walk or jog to the first check mark, start from the check mark with the takeoff leg or start with both feet on the check mark with the first stride being taken with the lead leg. If the second mark is used in the runup it should be hit with the takeoff foot.

If the high pole carry is used in the first phase of the run, the carry must be adjusted in the second half so that the pole is in a horizontal position four strides before takeoff.

The Plant

The last four strides before takeoff should be fast. The faster the controlled stride, the faster the execution of the plant and takeoff. The pole is planted in the last two strides. The movement into the box begins when the takeoff leaves the runway in the next to last stride. The pole should be moved forward close to the vaulter's body. It is imperative to avoid a sideways plant and a back lean at the plant. This action

reduces speed which is essential in an effective vault. The following is recommended to develop a smooth, rhythmic plant.

With the left foot forward and the pole held in proper carrying position, the vaulter steps forward with the right foot moving the pole forward and upward. As the left foot hits the ground the pole should be at a position above and in front of his head. The right arm should be fully extended. Repeat the same drill, but now jump off the ground with the left foot. The plant begins on the last two strides of the run.

Have the vaulter place the tip of the pole on the ground in front of him. He takes off with his left foot, driving his right knee forward, passing the pole on the right side. (Figure 6) He should hold on to the pole as he vaults forward, facing the same direction as the takeoff. Repeat several times.

The vaulter repeats plant, but now he uses a four-stride running approach, starting the run with his takeoff foot forward. Repeat several times, each time raising his grip one or two inches. Soon the grip will be one or two feet above the highest height he can reach with the pole standing vertically in the box. Now increase the run to six strides and repeat, again raising his handhold.

With the handhold several feet above the highest standing grip he can reach, the vaulter increases his run to eight strides. The vaulter must always take off with his left foot vertically beneath his right hand. He should have a vertical impulse at takeoff, leading with a bent right knee, before going into the swing phase. He then rocks back, bringing his knees as close to his hand grip as possible.

The takeoff practice should develop a strong forward movement of the lead leg, the thigh of which must be parallel to the pole when the takeoff action is completed. During takeoff the eyes should be focused on a specific spot as the upper body moves toward the pole with the hips remaining in position. A top arm stretched and a lower arm bent at a 90 degree angle provide the active resistance against the pole.

The Swing

The swing is begun shortly after the takeoff by dropping the lead leg slightly. The takeoff leg, which has remained in a stretched position, catches up with the lead leg. Both legs begin a fast upward swing. The hips as well as the legs must be lifted. The fast upward lift of the leg increases the pole bend during the swing.

He should think of getting his hips higher than his shoulders. The right arm remains extended through the rock back. As he improves, he can give himself additional height by pulling downward through the length of the pole as his knees come to his handhold, and as the pole approaches the vertical.

The straightening of the body in preparation for bar clearance must be synchronized with the straightening of the pole. The vaulter must remain close to the pole and parallel to it as the pole "works" for the vaulter.

The turning movement begins when the shoulder (usually left) reaches the height of the left hand. This movement is assisted by a turning of the legs and arms.

Bar Clearance

If the arms have been correctly used in the phases described, the vaulter will be brought into a vertical position with the head down as bar clearance begins. The bending of the hips and the crossing of the bar accompanied by the pushoff from the top arm contribute to the flyaway method of clearance. The legs should be kept together and the head should not be lifted too soon. The arms should be raised over the head, not thrown up over the head.

The jumper arches the back to clear the bar, going over head first (see back). Do not reach out over the bar with the hands. As the torso clears, the jumper should whip up the knees and feet. The arms are held next to the side. When the hips are clear, it is helpful to raise the arms and flex the hip which in turn helps to raise the feet. Again, maintain speed and rhythm throughout the entire technique.

Practice Hints

1. Raising the center of mass as high as possible over the bar is the most important factor in the flop. Thus, the techniques of the approach, plant and takeoff should be practiced much more than the technique of bar clearance. (Work on leg and arm lift and bounding drills on the grass.)
2. If the jumper is hitting the bar on the way up (caused by reaching maximum height too soon, the takeoff is too close to the bar.
3. Conversely, if the jumper is hitting the bar on the way down, the takeoff is too far from the bar.
4. To eliminate leaning into the bar, press the inside shoulder up.
5. The first two or three strides of the approach are very important and determine a consistent pattern. This is where the rhythm of the approach run is developed.

6. The full run should be established immediately. The long run stride pattern, acceleration, curve and rhythm can be developed (7-11 strides).
7. A short run of 4-6 strides should be established for working on preparation for takeoff and takeoff techniques.
8. The jumper should practice the last two strides of the short run for quickness in the last step and, at the same time, remain relaxed and maintain the momentum developed in the run.

SECTION
VII

The Throws

SHOT PUT

A good shot put performance demands an appropriate blend of speed and quickness, a high degree of explosive power, great strength, good height, and motivation. Effective shot putting involves a simple and natural movement coupled with a coordinated drive of the legs and thrust of the back with arm delivery.

The logical order of progression in practice of the shot put should be: (1) developing the proper grip, (2) developing the correct stance and making the delivery, (3) practicing the glide across the circle, and (4) integrating the putting technique.

The Grip

The shot is held in the hand so that it presses against the base of the fingers. This reduces tension and permits the full range of the fingers in the snap-release. The fingers may be placed together or spread slightly.

The shot may be gripped by placing the first three fingers together and using the small finger and thumb to hold it in position. The wide finger spread is recommended for putters with small hands. The spread should not be exaggerated to the point that the fingers cannot be used to give impetus to the shot. Beginners should carry the shot lower down in the palm of the hand until greater strength is developed.

The Power Position and Delivery

The right foot is placed in the middle of the circle at approximately a 45 degree angle to the flight of the shot. The knee is slightly flexed with the body weight over the right leg for maximum drive. The right leg is extended vigorously to begin the force which moves up the leg, to the hips, to the trunk, to the arm for the final delivery with a snap of the wrist.

The left leg serves as a brace against which the force is exerted. The foot of the left leg is against the toe board. The right foot remains on the surface and continues to provide power in the delivery.

Early practice of the delivery should be done in a correct stance at the front of the circle. The delivery is a sequence of coordinated movements from the foot to the tip of the fingers.

The Glide

The glide is used to travel from the rear of the circle to the correct position for delivery. It begins by standing at the rear of the circle with the back to the direction of the put. The glide must begin with the athlete in good balance.

From the erect, relaxed, balanced position at the rear of the circle, the athlete lowers the head and shoulders by flexing the hips to a position in which the back is nearly horizontal. The eyes are focused on a spot directly behind the circle, the right knee is bent to a point which will give the greatest lifting power and rocks forward until the weight is over the ball of the right foot.

Momentum is generated by moving the weight of the body toward the toe board. Additional momentum is gained by driving off the right leg and ball of the foot as the left leg engages in a piston-like motion.

The piston-like motion is achieved by bringing the knee forward, then extending it vigorously straight back toward the toe board. The hips should remain low. The entire action should be made with the legs rather than with the upper body. The left leg, as indicated, lands against the toe board to the left of center of the circle.

At the end of the glide and turn in position for delivery, the stance should be the same as the one assumed at the front of the circle during earlier practice sessions without the glide.

The Reverse

The purpose of the reverse is to prevent a foul after completion of a powerful delivery. The reverse is completed by switching the feet. The rear foot replaces the front foot by placing the outer edge of the rear foot at the inner edge of the toe board. The body weight is shifted back after the landing, but not until all power is delivered.

THE DISCUS

Execution of the basic skills in the "discus throw" defies the definition of a throw in which the elbow leads the object being thrown. In the release of the discus, the athlete appears to be slinging the object. In future discussions in this chapter, remember the concept of the sling when throwing is mentioned.

The logical order of progression in attempting to perfect the discus throw is: (1) developing the proper grip, (2) developing the correct stance and release, (3) practicing the controlled spin across the circle, and finally (4) integrating all aspects of the throw into an acceptable pattern.

Three basic mechanical principles must be adhered to in executing the throw:

1. The body is moving forward over the circle at the moment of release. However, the feet are stationary in the "power position" as the upper body continues to move forward.
2. The path of the discus is parallel to the path of the body during the acceleration period in the spin. Defying this principle will lead to a loss of speed in the throwing arm.
3. The discus should be kept as far away from the vertebral column as possible to provide for the longest possible radius of rotation. By keeping the arm fully extended the thrower can exert a longer pull and thereby generate a longer period of force.

The Grip

The grip will vary with individuals according to hand size and experience. Developing the proper grip should begin by placing the discus

in the non-throwing hand. Then place the discus in the throwing hand so that its circumference rests on the last joints of the fingers. Only the first joints of each finger should be over the edge of the discus. The thumb is placed at the edge of the discus but does not come over the rim. The thumb in this position is pressed against the discus.

Basically there are two ways the fingers can be placed on the discus: (1) the fingers and thumb are spread apart and (2) the index finger and middle finger are placed next to each other with the other two fingers and thumb spread out on the discus. (See Illustration).

Release from the Hand

Primarily the discus is released off the index finger and rotates in a clockwise manner (for a right-handed thrower). It is important to develop a release that will result in a smooth spin which will stabilize the discus in flight.

Drill: Rolling the discus (using the lines on a football field or any lines on the gym floor). The athlete takes 4 to 5 steps carrying the discus extended down at his side, swings and releases the discus down the line. (The action is similar to a bowling movement.) The discus should travel in a straight line. This movement is essentially the same as a release from the throwing position in that it comes off the index finger last.

Vertical throw into the air. The objective of this drill is to teach proper technique in releasing the discus and spin control. The athlete should assume a stride stance with the leg opposite the discus forward. The discus should be held with palm facing the leg with the arm completely straight. The arm should swing in a pendulum motion backward and forward then upward. At the point of the upward swing just prior to the arm being in a horizontal position the discus should be "squeezed" by the throwing hand and then released with a counterclockwise spin into the air. The discus should land on the ground. Initially, the discus should be thrown only a few feet above the head. As experience is gained and more skill is developed, the knees and waist may be flexed to generate more power for a higher toss.

The Stance and Release

1. Place rear foot in middle of ring at an angle of approximately 45 degrees or less.
2. The front foot should be comfortably spread in direction of throw. (A little wider than shoulder width.)
3. The front foot can range from being on the bisecting line to approximately 8 inches off the center line. The relationship of the feet is the toe of the front foot in line with the heel of the rear foot. (Heel/toe relationship.)

The Swing

The preliminary swings establish the rhythm of the throw. They should be free, continuous and smooth flowing. The discus should sweep through the widest orbit around the body and as far back as possible. If the swings are too fast and forceful, rhythm, balance and position are destroyed.

Power Position

Place the right foot on the middle of the circle. Rotate the foot so that the toe is pointing at about 10 o'clock. Weight is balanced on the flexed right leg. The left foot should land in the pocket. The toe of the left foot should be just about even with the right heel if not back a little, leg flexed slightly and relaxed. The feet are a little more than shoulder width apart. This is done so that when the athlete rotates his hips, he will be open to the throwing area. The hips constitute the direction of the discus.

In the learning stages it is advisable to teach the delivery from the power position without a reverse. Many beginners use a reverse and end up throwing with the arm, leaving out the all-important legs and hips.

Action

1. At the end of the second backswing, squat down over the rear leg with the waist bent forward slightly.
2. Most of the weight of the body should be over the rear leg.
3. The discus arm is held high and as far back as possible.
4. The free arm should wrap around the front of the chest.
5. The delivery starts with an extension of the elbow of the free arm and a horizontal swing backward of the free arm. It sweeps around extended until the hips are halfway turned forward. At this time it shortens, putting a great stretch on the front of the chest. From this stretched position the muscles of the chest can act more forcefully.
6. A split second after the free arm starts its movement the legs and hips start their drive forward and around, dragging the discus behind.
7. When the hips and shoulders are facing the front, the front foot and leg extend while the throwing arm strikes. It is at this point that the hip action begins to rise; however, the thrower must think predominantly of a circular action.
8. As the arm strikes, the discus should be elevated to approximately shoulder level and should be flat.
9. In the release the discus should rotate off the index finger in a smooth spinning flight (clockwise for right-hand throwers). The angle of release is approximately 39 degrees and will vary according to the wind direction. The projection will be slightly higher if the wind is behind the thrower.

The Controlled Spin

Both feet are at the back of the circle. The left foot is placed on the center line instead of having to straddle the line. Starting off in this position allows the athlete to use more of the circle and to use more of a circular motion, creating a greater velocity of the discus.

SECTION VIII

Building A Training Program

The Psychological and Physiological Dimensions of Training

Five things should be considered prior to setting up the program:
1. The running program during the summer months.
2. The nature and extent of any weight-training program.
3. The nature and extent of any off-season competition in other sports.
4. The nature and extent of any injuries that may have been sustained during the summer, or which may have lingered from the previous season.
5. The event or events for which the athlete will train.

The athlete must have a definite understanding about the essential facts concerning proper care of the body. It is important to use an objective approach to health facts for the well-conditioned body, rather than a long list of training rules which are almost impossible to implement. While there are some fundamental health facts which have a definite influence on the performance of an athlete, most of the "training rule" lists include items which are basically psychological. To break one of the published rules often would have little effect upon the performance of the athlete, but it may have serious social and emotional implications.

Goals for the athlete should be high and he/she should be dedicated to the spartan simplicities.

Psychological Considerations

The athlete is not only the sum of his physical qualities but also an intricate combination of psychological conditions. However great his/her speed or strength, these may be rendered useless if there is not an effective combining of the physical and psychic qualities at the most appropriate moment. The athlete is a complicated combination of both.

One of the most fundamental principles is that psychical conditions change and psychical states have varying effects upon the track and field performer.

"Psyching" is a term frequently used by athletes. It refers both to the performer's influence upon the opponent and the ability to prepare for competition. "Psyching" takes many forms. It varies from simply ignoring an opponent and exuding confidence in the preliminary warm-up to dropping hints which start an opponent thinking negatively and running for second. A great performance has tremendous "psyching" influence. Psychical effects vary according to strength and length, and they are difficult to explain.

The important thing for the athlete to understand is that these psychical states may be useful or undesirable. Some useful states — feelings, emotions, or attitudes — are: (1) interest, (2) readiness, (3) self-confidence, (4) enthusiasm, (5) perseverance. Practice sessions should be organized to keep interest and enthusiasm high. Keep it "short and sweet."

I once read a statement by John Michael Landy (Australia) written at the height of his performances as a premier miler in the mid-fifties. He stated, "I am sure it is not necessary to train five hours daily to win an Olympic title. Even a daily average of an hour and a half, with absolute concentration, could achieve the desired result."

The ability to sustain an intense workload is diminished if the athlete has lost the zest for practice. Too frequently, I am afraid, this condition is brought on by an hour and a half workout extended to three hours. Should it be necessary to work over an extended period of time, vary the program, change the work pace, and put a little spice in the session.

Physiological Considerations

The athlete's training in track and field is largely a self-determined responsibility. While the coach may direct practice routine, the athlete is responsible for diet, sleep and rest.

There are a wide variety of training patterns which the athlete can choose to achieve a physiological base. A good understanding of the effects of activity upon the human body is absolutely essential in planning the individual workout. Athletes respond differently to weight training or other systems. Select the plan which is best for you. Slavish imitation may prove detrimental.

Some General Principles

1. Perform exercises correctly in terms of the results desired. If an exercise cannot be performed correctly for the desired repetitions (usually a minimum of 8), reduce the amount of weight.
2. Increase repetitions each workout until 10 to 12 can be performed. Five to ten pounds should be added to the load when repetitions can be easily handled and performed with less full effort.
3. Rest 2 to 3 minutes between exercises.
4. Schedule weight-training workouts with three factors in mind:
   a. alternate days for more effective workouts.
   b. space exercises during workout.
   c. train and do not strain.

Perform the exercises in a proper sequence. Shift the demands on muscle groups during workouts. This is accomplished by changing emphasis. Exercise the legs and the back, then the chest and arms. The workouts may vary from 30 minutes to 2 hours.

Muscular strength and endurance increases when exercises are repeated against increased resistance. The following principles should be remembered:

1. Progressively increase the total load.
2. Progressively increase the total time given to a load.
3. Progressively increase the repetitions against a constant and known resistance.
4. Progressively increase the speed of the performance.
5. Increasing the body weight without an increase in strength is bad. Always continue strength-building exercises in combinations with weight-control measures.
6. Performing exercise before proper warm-up has been completed is risky.
7. Continuing intense weight-training immediately prior to competition is not desirable. It is essential to allow muscle fibers to repair and recover from soreness.

Every athlete may not be able to find a Training Center. Improvise your own bar weights to use at home in the basement or back yard. Use of free weights can be of great value in developing the body.

Chart I

Suggested Exercises for Upper Body

Exercise	Weight	Repetitions	Starting Position	Movement	Complementary Action	Purpose
Curls	30-40 or 75-90 pounds	8-12	Supinated grasp (palms forward); shoulder width; raise weight to hang across thigh; body erect.	Raise bar to chest by flexing lower arm. Lower to starting position.	Inhale as bar is raised; exhale as bar is lowered.	To develop biceps and forearm muscles
Reverse Curls	30-40 or 75-90 pounds	8-12	Pronated grasp (palms toward thigh); others, same as above.	Same as above.	Same as above.	To develop forearm muscles
French Curls	20-30 or 35-50 pounds	8-12	Place the barbell across the shoulders at the base of the neck; spread feet to shoulder width; hold body erect; keep the elbows higher than the barbell.	Push weight straight up by extending the arms; lock the elbows; lower to a starting position.	Same as above.	To develop tricep muscles
Wrist Curls	35-45 or 65-90 pounds	8-12	Sit on the bench with the weights in the hands; hold palms up; rest the forearms on the thighs; extend the wrists past the knees.	Allow weights to roll down the hand; grasp with fingers; bring weight back into the hands and bend the wrist toward body.		To develop fingers, wrist, forearm muscles
Pullovers	20-40 pounds	8-12	Lie flat on the back; extend the arms fully and place the barbell on the floor; catch it with a shoulder-width grasp.	Lift the weight straight up until it is directly over the chest; lower to a starting position.	Exhale as the bar is brought over the chest; inhale as the bar is lowered to the floor.	To develop upper arms and chest

Chart II
Suggested Exercises for Abdomen, Back, and Trunk

Exercise	Weight	Repetitions	Starting Position	Movements	Complementary Action	Purpose
Trunk Bender	40-90 pounds	8-12	The barbell should be placed across the shoulders at the base of the neck, the feet should be shoulder width; the body should be held erect.	Bend forward from the hips until the trunk is parallel to the floor; return to the starting potition.	Exhale as you bend forward; inhale on return.	To develop trunk muscles
Rowing	50-100 pounds	8-12	The legs should be straight; bend forward at the hips until the body is parallel to the floor; the feet should be spread. Grasp the barbell at the shoulder with the palms toward the legs; keep the head up.	Pull the barbell straight up to touch the chest; lower to the starting position. Lift with the arms only.	Inhale as you lift the barbell; exhale as the barbell is lowered.	To develop the upper back muscles and the arms
Dead Lift	80-120 pounds	8-12	Stand close to the barbell with the feet slightly wider than the shoulder; keep the trunk bent forward and the knees straight. Grasp the bar with an overhand grip; slightly wider than shoulder.	Raise the trunk upward and backward to an erect position; raise the bar to the thighs. Do not bend the knees. Lower the bar until it touches the floor; stand erect.		To develop the lower and the upper trunk muscles
Trunk Flexes	5-10 pounds	25-100	The feet should be placed under the bar; the barbell plate should be behind the head.	Flex the trunk with an alternate left and right twist.		To develop the abdominal muscles.

Chart III
Suggested Exercises for Legs, Ankles, and Back

Exercise	Weight	Repetitions	Starting Position	Movements	Complementary Action	Purpose
Three-Quarter Squats	70-110 pounds	20-40	The barbell should be placed across the shoulders at the base of the neck; the feet should be spread shoulder width; the toes should be pointed outward.	Flex the leg to three-quarters of a full squat; return to the starting position.	Inhale on squat; exhale on stand.	To develop the exterior muscles of the legs and the back
Bench Squat	70-110 Pounds	20-40	Same as above.	Flex legs; lower hips to the bench. Keep the heels on the floor.	Inhale on sit; exhale on stand.	To develop the thigh and the hip muscles
Straddle Hops	80-125 pounds	20-40	The barbell should be placed across the shoulders at the base of the neck; the feet should be together.	Jump to straddle with feet at shoulder width; keep toes pointed straight forward, head up; return to the starting position.		To develop the muscles of the leg
Leg Press	80-150 pounds	10-20	Lie on the back with the thighs and the lower leg flexed; support the barbell on the feet (use assistant).	Extend the legs against resistance; return to the starting position.		To develop the leg extensor muscles